'Hello again' because although the title may not give any hint, tl
where my first book, *The Mandolin Tutor*, left off. So I'll flatter my   ...ought that
some of you reading this might already have worked your way through that volume and
have decided to come back for more! If that's the case, thank you!

If you're not one of those people, then thank you anyway!

There's a stage in mandolin playing where you feel you've conquered the basics: first
position feels comfortable, you can get from one end of a tune to the other without the
rhythm falling apart (maybe even in public), and perhaps you're even getting
sort-of-vaguely-OK-ish at reading standard music notation. If that's where you are, then I
hope *Mastering The Mandolin* will be well suited to you.

You might have reached this point through a short, sharp burst of enthusiasm and are keen
not to lose momentum. If so, more power to your plectrum! But no matter what our level of
competence, we all experience that 'plateau feeling' from time to time: a year or more
seems to have gone by and we haven't learned any new tunes, we feel in a rut with our
technique. None of us likes it, but it is common and shouldn't be cause for undue worry. If
that's where you are, I hope this will provide that nudge of inspiration to get your mandolin
playing on the move again.

I've tried to make the book general in it's approach. By that, I mean that it's not geared to
any one musical style; rather, it's a resource of technical advice that you can either work
your way through from front to back, or dip into at will. You can apply the ideas and
suggestions you find here to whatever you like to play on the mandolin, and I hope you'll
find help and inspiration whatever your musical preferences. While it's not a repertoire
book, I've chosen musical examples that I personally find stimulating and satisfying to play.
In a couple of cases, I've also included tunes that people specifically requested, ones which
fortunately lent themselves to demonstrating a particular technical challenge.

Ideally, you should use this book with a sympathetic teacher (those last two words should
always go together), but I realise how few mandolin teachers there are, so as always, I've
written it with the lone student firmly in mind.

Good luck!

CONTENTS

HELLO AGAIN   3

1   THE LEFT HAND 'ATTITUDE'   6
     ..... exercises 1, 2 & 3 - The Bluebell Polka .....

2   THE FOURTH FINGER   10
     ..... I Saw Three Ships (G) - I Saw Three Ships (A) - The Cuckoo's Nest -
     Maloney's Last Glass .....

3   USING OPEN STRINGS   14
     ..... Exercises 4 & 5 - The Flea Hop - Eigg Dance .....

4   ARIA   16

5   CLOSED POSITION   18
     ..... Exercises 6, 7 & 8 - Three Blind Mice (A) - Three Blind Mice (B♭) -
     La Marche des Moutons (G) - La Marche des Moutons (A♭) -
     Turkey in the Straw .....

6   SHIFTING POSITION   22
     ..... Exercises 9, 10, 11, 12 & 13 .....

7   TUNES WITH SHIFTS   24
     ..... Nevsky Prospekt - The Three Sea Captains - Sonatina in C (excerpt) .....

8   ADJACENT FIFTHS   27
     ..... Bunch of Fives .....

9   THE MATHEMATICIAN   30

10   SIMPLE HARMONIES   32
     ..... Buy Broom Besoms (simple & adorned) -
     Cannily, Cannily (simple & adorned) - Speed the Plough -
     The Artful Lodger - The Trumpet Hornpipe .....

11   MORE COMPLEX HARMONIES   38

> ..... *March of the Worker Ants - Swan's Waltz - Hammer & Nails -*
> *Kyoto Road .....*

12   THE RIGHT HAND   42

> ..... *plectrums - standard grip - tone production .....*

13   PENCIL GRIP   45

14   TREMOLO   46

> ..... *Exercises 14, 15 & 16 - Lovely on the Water - Song of the Birds -*
> *Lark in the Clear Air .....*

15   DOUBLE STOPPED TREMOLO   50

> ..... *Santa Lucia .....*

16   BUNCHES & EXTENTIONS   52

> ..... *Along The Grove - Vivaldi Mandolin Concerto (excerpt 3rd mvnt) -*
> *Exercise 17 - Vivaldi Mandolin Concerto (excerpt 1st mvnt) .....*

   SCRAPBOOK   55

> ..... *a few photographs .....*

17   HARMONIES AGAIN   56

> ..... *The Captain's Apprentice - I'm Doon For Lack o'Johnny .....*

18   MIND OVER MANDOLIN   58

> ..... *Jump the Gun .....*

19   DUET   60

> ..... *June Apple .....*

20   SWINGAROLA   62

THE LEFT HAND 'ATTITUDE'

We're going to start by playing through a few stimulating little exercises to get the left hand CD ref loosened up and to make sure its position or 'attitude' is good. This will recap on an important fundamental principle of mandolin playing. It's something I've discussed in print before, but getting into bad habits really can be such a brake on your progress that I make no apology for bringing the subject up again.

Whether you sit or stand, the mandolin neck should not need support from the left hand. If you sit, this shouldn't be a problem. If you stand, use a strap.

Exercise 1

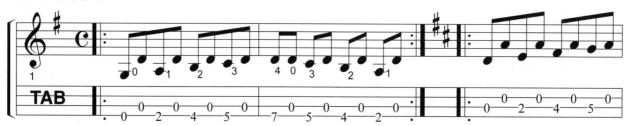

CD ref

Exercise 2

CD ref
CD ref

These exercises may not seem too difficult, but bear in mind that the important thing is not the fretted notes, but the open strings. Although *Exercise 1* is written in quavers (8th notes), try to give them more of a crotchet (quarter note) value, so each note sustains a little under the next. It's important that the open strings do not sound muffled; they should ring clear even though the adjacent string is being fingered.

If you found you were getting muffled open strings on the previous exercises, it's worth having a CD ref close look at these illustrations and spending time on your left hand position before you go further.

Don't be tempted to let the neck of the instrument sink into your palm (*Figure 1*). It's just about possible to survive in first position by playing like this, but the moment you start doing something more adventurous (the purpose of this book, after all!) and moving up the neck of the mandolin, you'll find yourself hampered. Rest the neck lightly between your thumb and the side of your first finger, roughly where it joins your hand. Now curl your left hand fingers round and play the strings. The final knuckle of each finger should hit the strings from directly above, perpendicular to the fingerboard and (this was the purpose of the previous exercises) without touching the adjacent strings.

You'll find the knuckles of your first finger in particular will be curled into quite a compact 'U' shape, the other fingers less so, and in some cases the fourth finger may almost have straightened out to reach a note.

Let your wrist fall. Don't consciously arch it, or flatten it, or push it into any position you think it ought to be, just let gravity take hold and don't think about it too much!

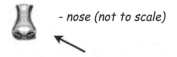 - *nose (not to scale)*

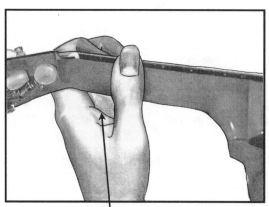

Figure 1

Don't let the neck of the mandolin sink into your hand. It should only touch the sides of your thumb and first finger.

Although we've not ventured higher up the neck of the mandolin so far, we have used the fourth finger to some degree in the exercises we've done. We'll concentrate more on it in the coming pages, but for now try *The Bluebell Polka*. It involves using the little finger on that high *b'* in some prominent places. Make sure it rings out loudly and cleanly!

The opening flourish of grace notes can be tricky, but follow the plectrum directions indicated and all should be well.

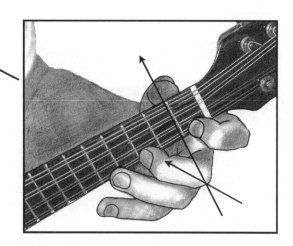

Figure 2

Notice from the arrows how the fingers are not square on to the fingerboard, but pointing more or less up towards your nose (added as an afterthought so you get the idea).

The Bluebell Polka

trad arr S Mayor

ef 10

THE FOURTH FINGER

CD ref

The reason we talk about the 'attitude' instead of the 'position' of the left hand is because string players also talk of playing 'in positions'. This is a technical use of the word to indicate the range of frets that can be accessed by the left hand fingers without resorting to moving the hand up and down the neck. In other words, when we are playing in a 'position', our fingers are moving but our hand isn't, or at least only minimally.

On the mandolin, 'first position' refers to the range from the open string up to and including the 7th fret (this would be fretted with the fourth finger). So, on any one string, first position spans eight semitones, counting the open string which obviously doesn't need fingering.

Figure 3

Showing a typical first position left hand attitude. The first finger covers frets 1 & 2, the second frets 3 & 4, the third frets 5 & 6, and the fourth fret 7.

I Saw Three Ships (G)

trad arr S Mayor

CD ref

My book, *The Mandolin Tutor*, intentionally stopped short of including any material that ventured beyond first position. For as there are thousands of songs with just three chords, so there are thousands of tunes we can play in the two and a bit octaves from the open G string up to that top *b'* on the seventh fret of the E string. Many people can, and do, spend their whole lives playing within these parameters. If you're interested in playing traditional folk music this is easily possible. After all, virtually all fiddle tunes fall within first position, and if this is your main mission on the mandolin, fine! If you're interested in playing in other styles - classical, swing, whatever - it's almost certain that you'll be required to play further up the neck from time to time. I'd also suggest that even if you do spend ninety-nine percent of your life in first position you'll be able to play more fluently and convincingly if you've bothered to acquaint yourself with the entire mandolin neck.

It's usual in the stringed instrument world to describe 'second position', 'third position' and so on as the left hand moves up the fingerboard to get higher notes. For the moment at least, I'll aim to simplify matters by referring to all of these as 'closed position'. In closed position we would not generally be playing any open strings and consequently the fourth finger will be used much more.

Ah, the fourth finger! Its inherent weakness really is an obstacle as we try to play fluently higher up the neck. Don't feel abnormal or even unusual in having this condition; we all suffer it! So, we'll take this in stages. First of all, let's stay in first position but force ourselves not to use any open strings. If you've never made a conscious effort to strengthen your little finger this could quite literally be an arresting exercise. Fun too, I hope.

The tunes here and overleaf are simple, but the point is to watch the indicated fingerings carefully and use that fourth finger! The tablature really helps here. You're allowed to play through them using open strings just to get acquainted, but then follow the fingerings exactly and try to get your playing sounding as fluent as if you were using open strings.

I Saw Three Ships (A)

trad arr S Mayor

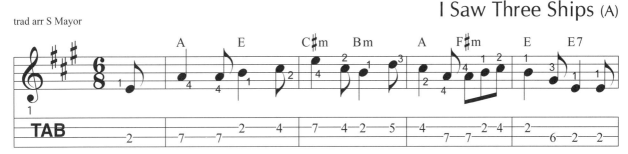

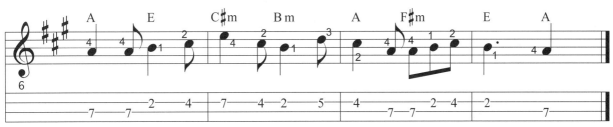

The Cuckoo's Nest

trad arr S Mayor

CD re

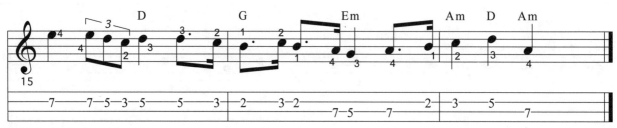

Maloney's Last Glass

S Mayor

Remember you're still supposed to be treating this tune as an exercise and should be avoiding the open strings. Try it like that to begin with, but you'll notice the tablature has reverted to 'normal' here and open strings are included. In an act of uncharacteristic kindness on my part, this is your reward for torturing yourself over the last few pages. So you can play this tune fairly briskly using open strings when you're familiar with it - it does sound good that way.

I've indicated a little decoration in the first few bars. You can play this with a quick hammer-on and pull-off. There's a fuller discussion of decoration in the book *New Celtic Mandolin* (see end catalogue page).

for this...   play this...

USING OPEN STRINGS

Well, I admit I was asking a lot in getting you to finger those last tunes in the way that I did, but it probably brought home to you just how neglected the fourth finger can be.

The frets are widest apart down this end of the neck, and consequently the stretch for all the fingers is greatest here. But just as most of us manage to drive a car safely without driving as we did on our test, so mandolin playing in the real world is a little more pragmatic. You may have noticed a difference in tone colour between a fingered note and an open string; it's not as marked as on a violin, but it's there. In places where this is going to be noticeable we can use our new found skill of fretting the seventh fret. Take a look at this simple phrase.

Exercise 4

It might seem obvious, but fretted notes stop ringing as soon as you lift your fingers; open strings don't. They either have to be intentionally damped or be stopped ringing by the next fretted note on the same string.

CD ref
CD ref

Sometimes we want to use this to our advantage, but at other times they will ring longer than we would ideally want them to, affecting the uniformity of tone colour within a phrase. In *Exercise 4* there's not really a problem playing the *a'* on an open string since the *b'* damps it. The top *e'* is more of an issue; if we play an open string there's a chance it will ring on under the *d'*, while playing it on the seventh fret gives the required length of note. You can hear the difference in tracks 17 (using the fourth finger) and 18 (using the open string) on the CD.

Below is a longer phrase with a recommended fingering for all possible open strings. Opposite are a couple of examples of what we'd normally think of as 'open-stringy' type tunes, but with some recommendations for using your little finger in exactly the way we're discussing.

Exercise 5

CD ref

S Mayor

with a strong swing

ef 20

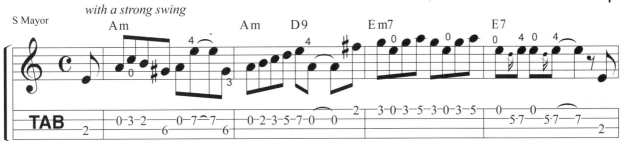

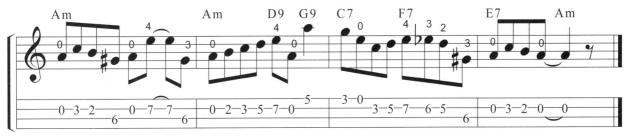

Eigg Dance

S Mayor

ef 21

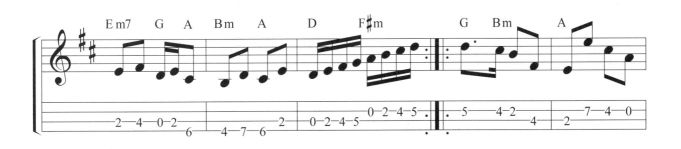

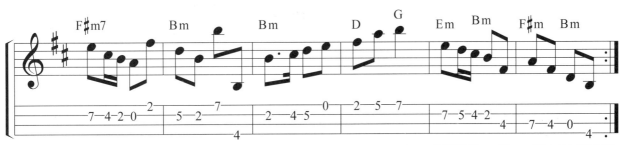

ARIA

G F Handel arr S Mayor

CD ref
CD ref

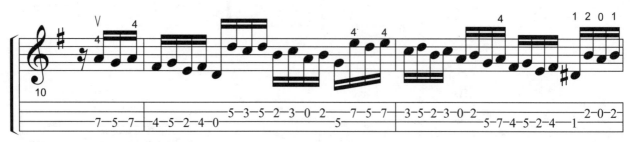

Here's a lovely piece by Handel; it acts as a great study for the left hand, all in first position. I've indicated where I would use the fourth finger to give the piece a uniformity of tone colour.

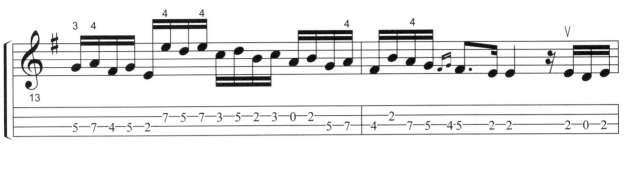

I've also shown at the end of bar 11 and start of bar 12 a slightly tricky bit of left hand work to get the *d#'* sounding positive.

CLOSED POSITION

If this is the first time you've tried anything like the tunes and exercises we've played so far, you've no doubt found them awkward, but at the same time you've probably achieved more than you realise. We'll try to build on this new found confidence in your little finger now, but first let's go right back to basics. Play up and down this simple scale of D major.

Exercise 6

CD ref
CD ref

Notice in the standard notation there are *two* left hand fingerings. The numbers above the notes show open strings and fingers 1, 2 and 3, but now try the fingering below. This will seem odd; you'll need to pretend you don't own a first finger. Still using the open strings where you can, your second finger will now fret the *e'* and *b'*, your third the *f#'* and *c#'*, and your fourth the *g'* and top *d'*. Try to make it sound equally fluent in both fingerings. As you play, try to memorise the tune (or scale in this case) and the fingering - in other words, the pattern you're playing. Incidentally, tracks 24 and 25 on the CD feature these alternative fingerings. You'll hear no difference between the two - but that's the whole point!

Now let's venture into closed position by moving up a semitone and playing a scale of Eb major; it's easily done if you think of the pattern you've just played with your second, third and fourth fingers. Move it one fret higher up the neck and imagine your first finger (now back in operation) to be a capo. By this I don't mean flatten it out across all four strings, but simply use it to play the notes of *eb'* and *bb'* on the first fret. Try it now.

Exercise 7

CD ref
CD ref

Now if you've managed it in Eb, it's no more difficult in E, or any other key for that matter. Don't get frightened by the number of sharps or flats in the key signature, just think of the pattern.

Exercise 8

CD ref

Now let's try the same idea with a tune, a really easy one just for demonstration purposes. You should be able to follow the same four stage process:

1. Play in first position using open strings where available and fingers 1, 2 and 3.
2. Play as above but using fingers 2, 3 and 4.
3. Think of, and memorise the pattern.
4. Move the pattern up a semitone (one fret) and bring in the first finger to cover notes on the first fret.

If you followed this process you should be able to play *Three Blind Mice* in B♭ with no trouble. Then try something more interesting, *La Marche des Moutons*, first in G then A♭ (turn the page).

Three Blind Mice (A)

Three Blind Mice (B♭)

La Marche des Moutons (G)

trad arr S Mayor

CD ref 31

La Marche des Moutons (A♭)

trad arr S Mayor

CD ref 32

You can look back at any of the tunes we were playing earlier, or any others you happen to know, and take them this one step further. Don't bother writing them down, just do it by ear.

❧ 20 ❧

Turkey In The Straw

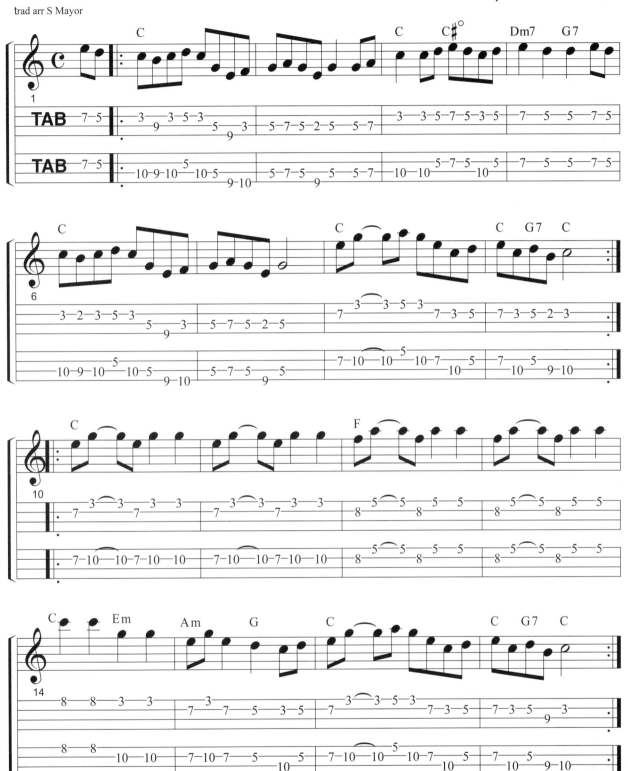

trad arr S Mayor

ref 33
ref 34

Here's a well known tune, but played unusually in C major and entirely in closed position. There are alternative tablature staves, each with a different fingering pattern, at different places on the mandolin neck. Both patterns allow you to play through the tune at exactly the same pitch without changing position. Start with your second finger for the upper tablature staff, or third for the lower.

SHIFTING POSITION

CD ref

The next step in stretching your ability on the mandolin is to become familiar with changing positions, that is, moving the left hand up or down the neck of the mandolin to reach the higher notes. Before we try it, I'm going to come back (again!) to your left hand attitude, and remind you to check the illustrations on page 8.

Changing position in the middle of a tune means moving the hand up or down the neck, and you're not going to be able to do that easily if you're holding it too hard and causing friction. Don't be tempted to oil it or use talcum powder or discarded dripping from the local fish and chip shop; lubricants are not the answer. In any case, they would find their way into the windings of the strings and ruin them.

Remember the weight of the mandolin *should not be taken by the left hand*. Think of the mandolin neck as a piece of wood that obligingly guides your fingers to where they ought to be; touch it as lightly, and as little as possible.

Now, without fingering any strings, try moving the hand up and down the neck and feel the minimal resistance.

Here are a few exercises in position changing; in all of them I've indicated precisely where the left hand should move.

Exercise 9

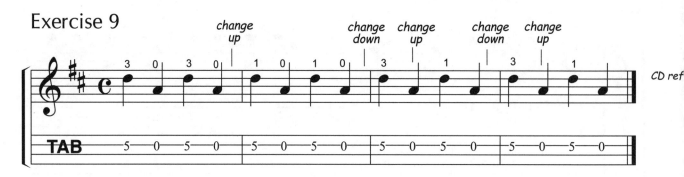

CD ref

The first exercise is simply an alternating *d'* and *a'*, but follow the fingering and make the shifts with the left hand at the appropriate places.

The next exercise is on similar lines but involves more fingers.

Exercise 10

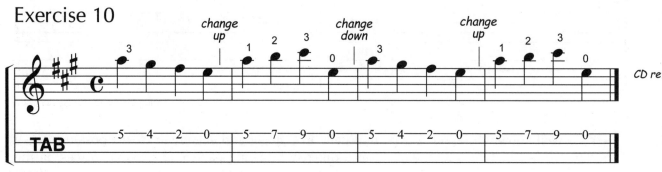

CD ref

By shifting positions, we can now play scales over two octaves; try these for starters. If you have a tape recorder, you can listen back to your playing without having to concentrate on what your fingers are doing. You should aim to get the position shifts inaudible, so listen hard!

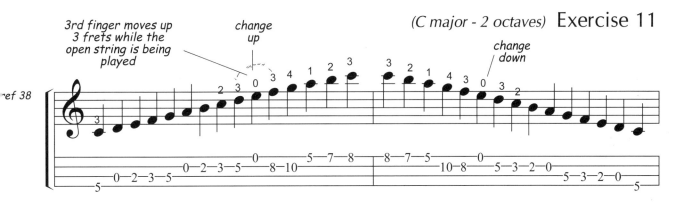

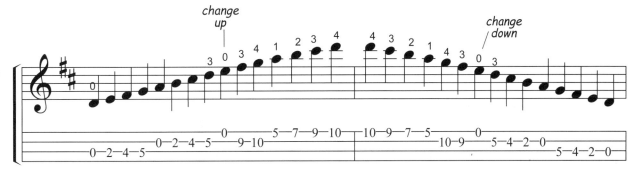

The two scales above involve up and down shifts with the third finger, but in each case there is a moment of 'breathing space' as we play the *e'* on the open string. The next scale involves a bigger jump, and although we still have that open *e'* for comfort, it involves switching from the third to the first finger and back again on the way down.

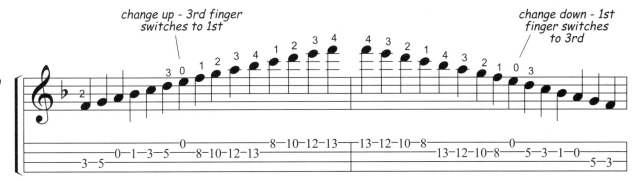

TUNES WITH SHIFTS

Now some tunes in which we can incorporate some position shifting. We don't always shift position just to reach the higher notes; by moving to a higher position on the same string (rather than crossing to a higher pitched string) we can gain a thicker tone colour, if that's what we want (and we do in *Nevsky Prospekt*).

Nevsky Prospekt

The Three Sea Captains (overleaf) is a gentle jig; no need to take it too fast. There's just one change up and one change down in the tune. Change up at the end of bar 17; you haven't got the luxury of an open string here but it's at the end of a long note so you should be able to do it smoothly. Change down on the open string at the start of bar 24.

The Three Sea Captains

Sonatina in C *(excerpt)*

L v Beethoven arr S Mayor

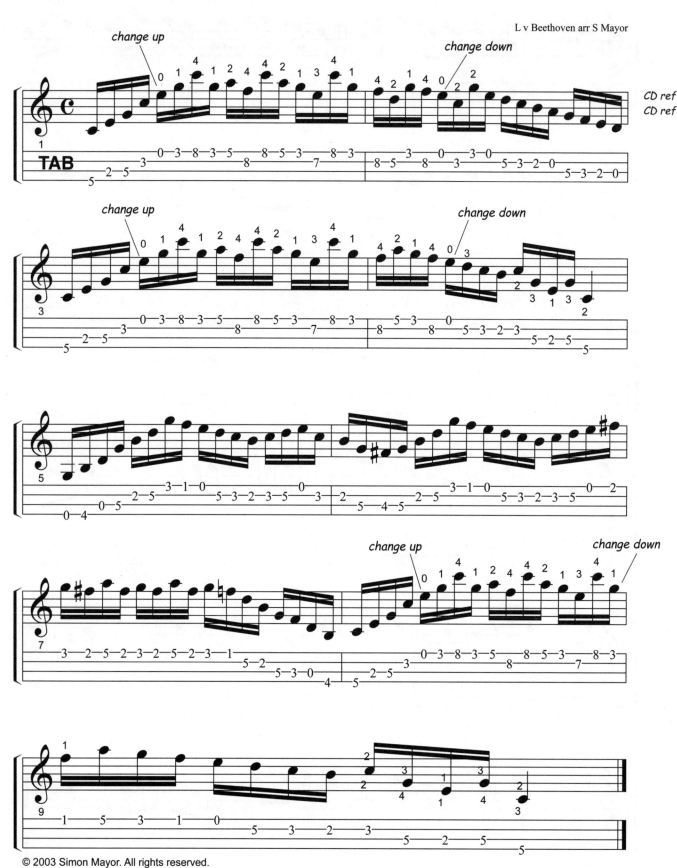

BEETHOVEN'S ADJACENT FIFTHS

(poor joke)

There's no getting away from it, adjacent fifths on a mandolin are a pain in the neck... or worse. Although this excerpt from one of Beethoven's few pieces for mandolin is mainly made up of scales and arpeggios, he throws in quite a few adjacent fifths to make it a little more difficult.

An example occurs in the very first bar where the high c' follows the f'. It's not a blisteringly fast tune, but it trots along a bit and we don't want to get into doing extensions (discussed more elsewhere) by playing both notes on the top string. In any case, that would mean an extra position shift. So there's nothing for it but to move the fourth finger across from the second to the first string as quickly as we can. You'll find that if you hop over with the tip of the finger you'll get a noticeable hiccup in the flow of the tune. The solution is in *Figure 4:* see how the finger stays on the f' but rocks over onto the c' so that for a moment the pad, rather than the tip of the finger, is covering both notes.

Try playing the phrase this way and it will sound a lot more fluent.

Figure 4

The fourth finger rocks backwards after it has played the f' to get the high c' with the pad of the finger.

Beethoven must have really loved mandolinists as he inflicts the same problem on us in bar 2 where the high g' follows the c'. We're on the second finger this time *(see Figure 5)* but the solution is the same: rock it over onto the top string rather than taking it off and on again.

If your fingers are big enough, you may be able to cover two strings at once without rocking. This is fine of course.

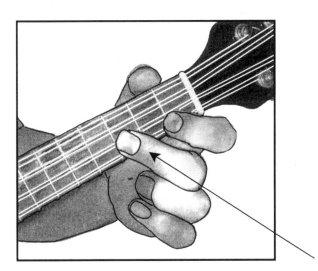

Figure 5

This time the second finger rocks over onto the top string g' after playing the c'.

Now look at the very last two notes of the piece: adjacent fifths going down rather than up. We can't rock a finger over to a lower string, so I've made a couple of suggestions shown in the alternative fingerings above and below those last five notes of bar 9. Either of these will maintain the flow of the piece but a good left hand attitude is essential in getting one finger tucked closely on top of the other.

The same choice happens at the end of bar 4, by the way.

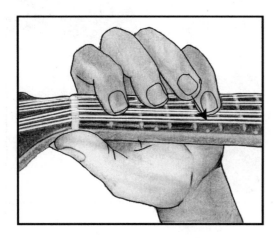

Figure 6

The second finger plays the high c', the fourth the g', and the first the e'.

The arrow shows third finger ready to play the low c'.

Figure 7

This is actually my preferred option... the second finger tucks on top of the third to get the low c'.

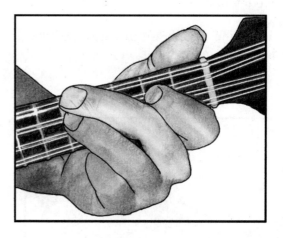

Bunch Of Fives

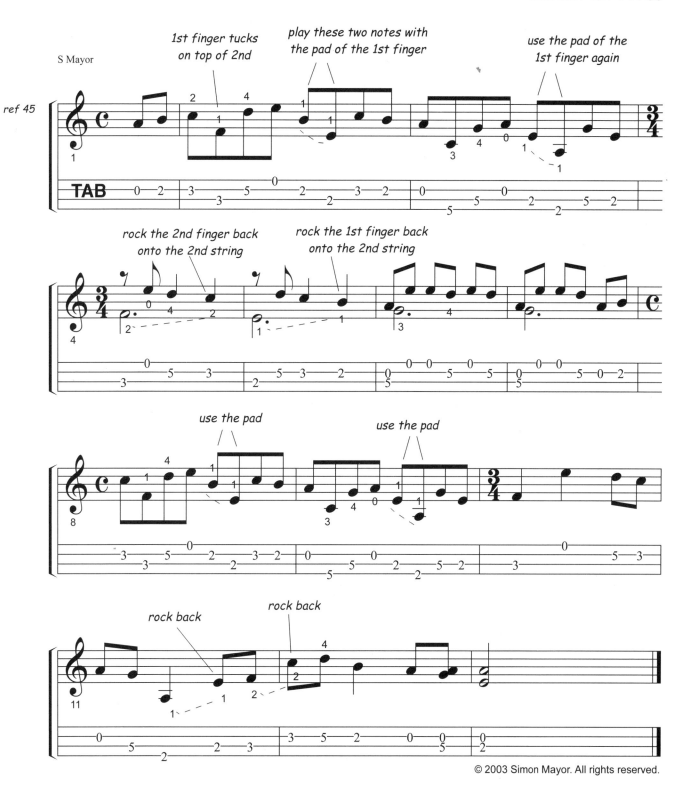

Here's a little tune written with the specific intention of driving you mad with these adjacent fifths. In some instances you'll be required to tuck the fourth finger in behind the third, on others you'll need to create a barré across two strings with the pad rather than the tip of a finger. These are shown by the dashed lines.

THE MATHEMATICIAN

J Scott Skinner arr S Mayor

CD ref 4
CD ref 4

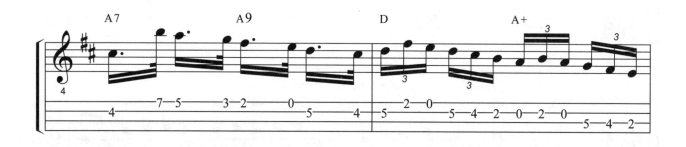

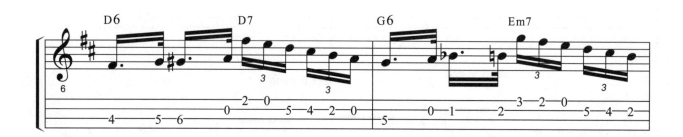

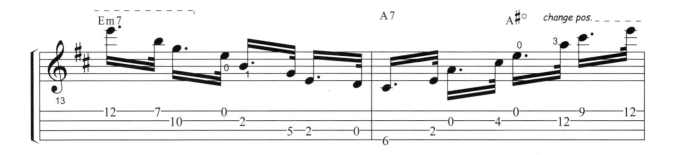

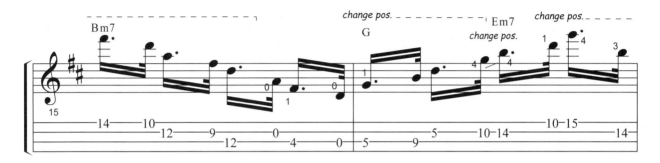

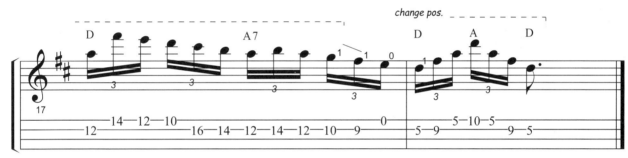

Deserving of a section to itself, this classic tune by Scott Skinner is both loved (and feared!) by Scottish fiddlers. It features some dramatic arpeggios in the second section that involve the left hand in considerable movement up and down the neck of the mandolin. These arpeggios can be made considerably easier if we make good use of open strings when shifting position. It's a technique that may not be a natural first line of attack to a fiddler, but take a close look at the *a'* in bar 10, the *e'* in bar 11, the *e'* in bar 12, the *e'* in bar 13 and so on. Each open string gives us that split second to move the left hand up or down the neck as required.

In bar 17 (the last three notes) I've indicated a quirky fingering where the first finger slides down from the *g'* to the *f#'*. It's an effect I quite like, but arguably not the most efficient for the left hand. Here's a more obvious fingering pattern for the last two bars which stays in one position:

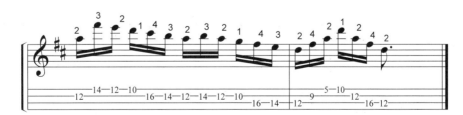

SIMPLE HARMONIES

Perhaps by now your left hand is sufficiently dexterous that you can play an up-tempo tune quite fluently. Don't lose sight of the fact that the mandolin need not be just a 'single line' instrument. In other words, something that just plays the tune over a guitar or piano accompaniment.

Buy Broom Besoms *(simple)*

trad arr S Mayor

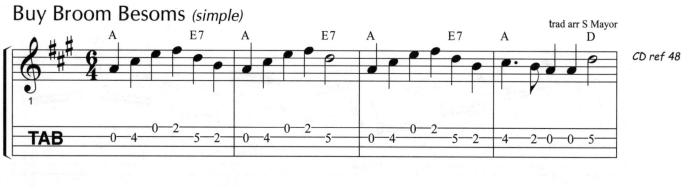

CD ref 48

Buy Broom Besoms *(adorned)*

trad arr S Mayor

CD ref 49

On these pages are a couple of traditional tunes shown first in their simple glory and then in what I've called adorned versions: exactly the same melody but brought to life by a little subtle harmony. Technically, the adorned versions are more difficult, and it's important to hold your left hand fingers down for the full note values as shown.

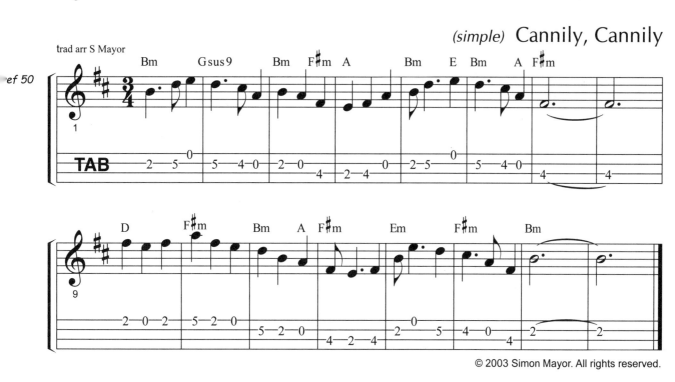

(simple) Cannily, Cannily

trad arr S Mayor

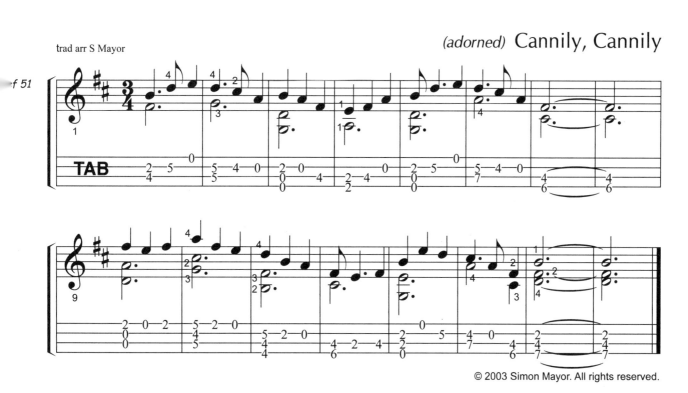

(adorned) Cannily, Cannily

trad arr S Mayor

Speed the Plough

Here are some more tunes in similar arrangements, this time I've given just the harmonised version. Play only the notes with stems up if you want the bare melody, and when you're familiar with the melody (it shouldn't take long) incorporate all the notes. Both tunes are in first position and there are no tricky fingerings... that comes later!

trad arr S Mayor

CD ref

The Artful Lodger

Before we get on to more complex harmonies, here's something in jig rhythm. *The Artful Lodger* is not a difficult tune, but as with all these pieces, give as much thought to the harmony notes as to the melody. Listen hard to yourself and make sure both lines are coming out cleanly. If not, take a look at your left hand attitude again!

The Trumpet Hornpipe

trad arr S Mayor

CD ref 55
CD ref 56

The Trumpet Hornpipe is a jaunty old tune. I've given some harmonies here that shouldn't be so difficult as to interrupt its flow.

Try to use the fourth finger rather than the open string where indicated in bars 8, 11 and 13.

There's a particularly nice section in bars 14 and 15 where the bass line (such as it is on a mandolin) descends the D string while the melody climbs the A string.

Incidentally, watch out at the end of bar 15 as the third finger has to push up from the *c#'* to the *d'* on the second string.

MORE COMPLEX HARMONIES

March of the Worker Ants

S Mayor

CD ref 57

These tunes are a little trickier than those on the previous pages.

In *March of the Worker Ants*, everything is in first position, and any difficult or non-obvious fingerings are marked. The idea is still the same, but instead of relying quite so much on open strings for the harmony notes, we're now doing more 'double stopping'. This term simply means fretting two strings at once.

Be particularly careful at the start of bar 9, where you should make sure the first finger is covering both the *e'* and, in anticipation, the *b'* (second quaver of the bar) right from the start.

A similar little tricky bit occurs in *Swan's Waltz* on the last beat of bar 5. The first finger should be barred across both the *e'* and the *a'* in anticipation of the first beat of the next bar.

Although it's a simple tune, *Swan's Waltz* is the first example of a melody and harmony line that are not directly in synchronisation. The two ring out under and over each other, and this means that it is vital that all notes are given their full value as written, otherwise the effect will be lost.

Swan's Waltz

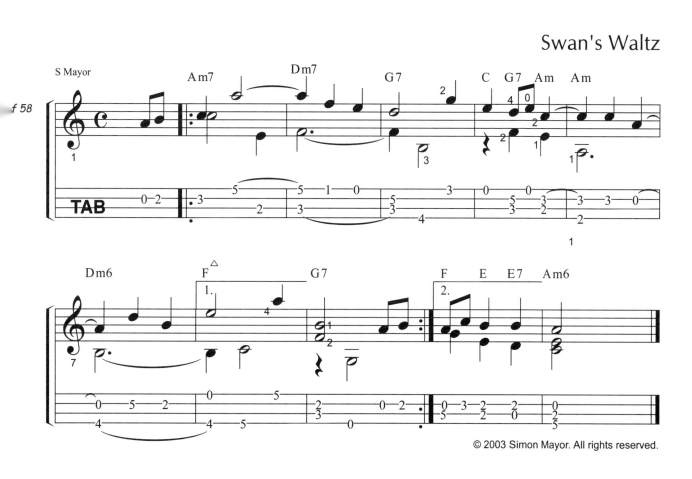

Hammer & Nails (overleaf) has many of the same technical characteristics as *Swan's Waltz*. It's in first position again, but even so there's some difficult left hand work. I've indicated some 'bunched' fingering (see pages 52 - 54) to make life a little easier in places.

Hammer & Nails

S Mayor

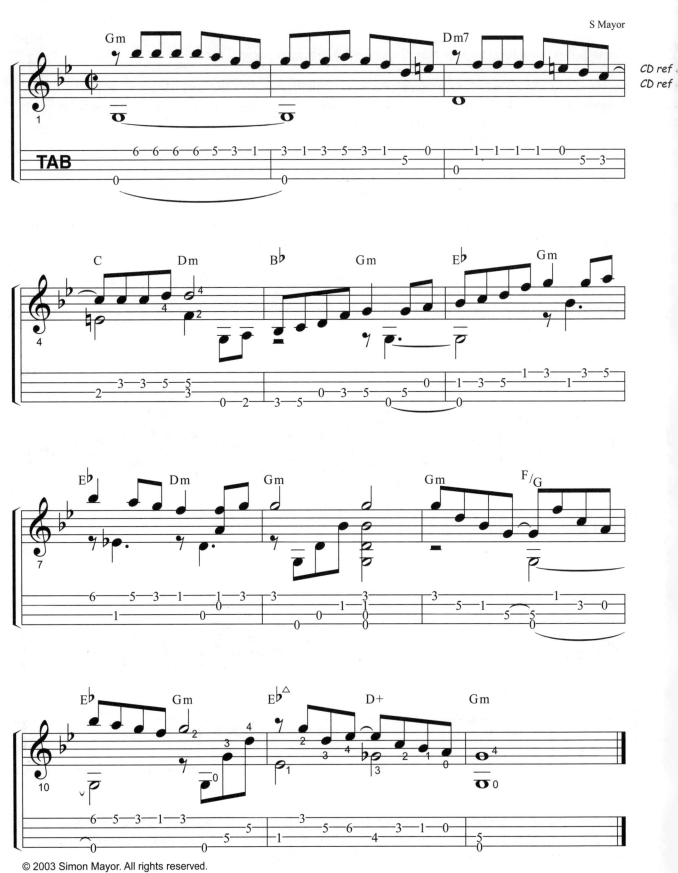

Kyoto Road

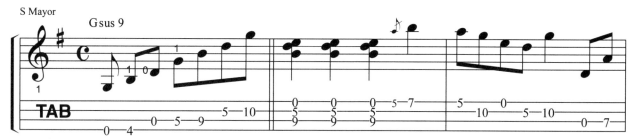
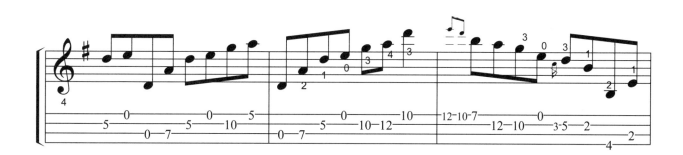
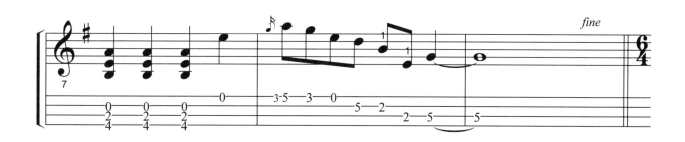
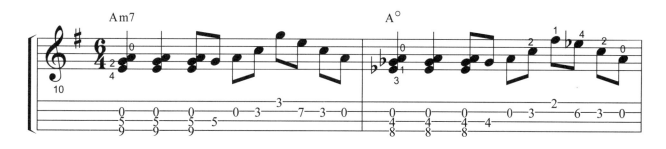
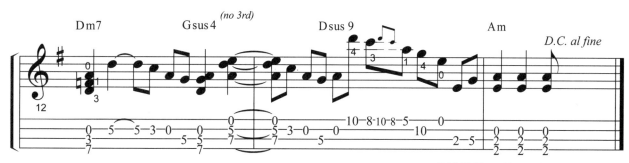

THE RIGHT HAND

It's all too easy to take the right hand for granted, but it's so much more than something that just gives energy to the strings, something that sets them vibrating. The right hand (assuming you're right handed of course) is crucial to good tone production, and there are so many factors involved.

Perhaps we should say right at the start that there is no single definition of 'good tone'. The sound you yearn for will depend on the style of music you're most interested in, which mandolinists you may want to emulate, and so on.

After your choice of an instrument your choice of plectrum is probably the most obvious thing to consider. In days of yore tortoiseshell was always the preferred material. It's now rightly banned, but there are still some mandolin players who have old tortoiseshell plectrums and have managed not to lose them. Some modern plastics are similar in their consistency, hard but not inflexible, and a fairly thin, pointed plectrum in such an imitation shell would be capable of producing a brilliant, penetrating tone. Match this with a good round-back instrument and you have the traditional formula for playing Italian style music.

At the other end of the scale are many American players who will use a heavy, thick plectrum. Opinion seems to vary as to the best shape, but many use well-rounded, almost circular ones. This, with a carved mandolin, is the favourite weapon for bluegrass.

There are other materials available; nylon is popular, and even polished stone (this is totally inflexible of course). We should also mention the German school of playing where a thick, rubbery plectrum is used on a round-back mandolin with flat-wound strings. The German design of mandolin is actually markedly different from the Italian, and in combination with flat-wound strings produces a softer, delicate tone which is unique in the mandolin world.

If you've not yet found the mandolin of your dreams, or the plectrum of your dreams, you should continue to experiment; it's considerably cheaper doing this with plectrums than with mandolins, but you should aim to find 'your sound'. Naturally, there are many shades of grey in all of this, and it's somewhere in this shady, plectral never-never land that your author is to be found. So, for better or worse, here's what I do.

My preferred shape is shown here; it's probably the most common shape of plectrum available. The ones I buy are usually stamped 'medium' and are around 0.8mm thick; this is probably the most common gauge available. I prefer plain, ordinary plastic, probably the most common material available. The one in the picture is black but red ones are louder. So there I am, Mr Average!

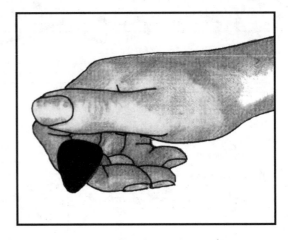

Figure 8

You should now start to think of the variety of tone colour you can produce from the plectrum. Hold it with about the same strength as you would use to hold a knife and fork - if you use cutlery - and leave just a millimetre or two protruding beyond the side of the first finger and the ball of the thumb. If you leave more than this the plectrum will flap about uncontrollably and you won't get 'good tone' by anyone's definition.

Hold it without even thinking about the mandolin. With a bit of luck you'll find your other fingers will naturally curl round in about the same arc as the first, effectively tucking themselves out of the way. We'll call this 'standard grip'.

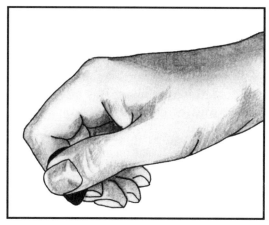

Figure 9

Showing 'standard grip'.

Now let your hand hover over the strings as you play. You may find your wrist resting lightly on the strings just behind the bridge, and you may find your second, third and fourth fingers brushing lightly against the top of the instrument (or scratchplate if it has one). These habits are fine up to a point, but be very careful not to damp the sound, as is almost certain to happen if you press hard with your wrist.

Figure 10

Don't rest your fourth finger on the mandolin or the bogey man will get you.

You'll also run the strong risk of introducing tension into your right hand. Some mandolinists, even experienced ones, rest their fourth finger on the top of the instrument as they play. The same arguments apply here, and I'd strongly advise against it.

In an ideal world your right hand should be free to move around, as this is a great way of varying the tone of the instrument. Play hard near the bridge and you'll get a piercing, brilliant sound. Now play over the end of the fingerboard and hear how much sweeter the tone is. While it's natural to crave some sort of an 'anchor' for the right hand, these techniques are simply not possible if the wrist is glued to the bridge, or the fourth finger to the top.

What's nice about the asymmetrically shaped plectrum is that you have a choice between a pointed and a rounded corner, and you can use both to differing effects. The pointed tip will give a bright tone, the rounded one a thicker sound. Try changing between the two now and you should be able to hear the difference.

The angle at which you strike the strings can also have a noticeable effect on tone. Have a look at these two illustrations. Again, you will have to experiment for yourself, but bear in mind that the *direction* of the stroke is the same in both cases. In *Figure 12* the plectrum is turned a little so that the string is not simply pressed and released by the face, but actually travels along the edge for a little way before being released. So, a greater amount of plastic is in contact with the string and the string is fooled into thinking it is being struck by a thicker plectrum. It's all over in nanoseconds, but believe me, the effect is noticeable.

Figure 11   *Figure 12*

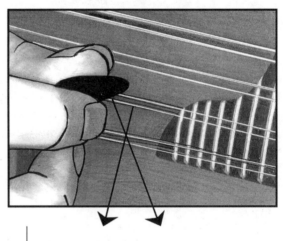

The plectrum is facing in the same direction as it is travelling - at right angles to the string.

Here the plectrum is still travelling in the same direction...

...but is facing at an angle to the string.

It may seem a small thing, but playing with what some would consider the 'wrong' corner may feel unnatural when you first try it. Similarly, an angled plectrum requires a little adjustment to your right hand attitude and may take a little getting used to. These things rarely fall into place overnight, but I hope you'll be sufficiently intrigued by the variety of tone colour you can get from just one piece of plastic that you'll persevere and continue to experiment.

When you do feel comfortable with all of this you'll find yourself using these techniques subconsciously in the middle of a piece for dramatic effect. Altering the plectrum angle mid-flow is not too difficult, but it's even possible to switch corners by flicking the plectrum round one third of a turn with your second finger. This is advanced stuff, and admittedly not 'mainstream' technique, but you may want to bear it in mind for future reference.

'PENCIL' GRIP

While we're considering the right hand I'll mention an alternative to standard grip which I call 'pencil grip'. It isn't widely used and I should say right at the start that it may not suit you, but I find it very useful for a couple of reasons.

Firstly, it's a very powerful grip and I use it where I need lots of volume; it's particularly good on an intense, screaming tremolo (more on tremolo coming up). Secondly, it gives me control over the stiffness of the plectrum, and so the tone it produces. If you're using a heavy gauge plectrum to begin with, then it's stiff by default, but for ones with some flexibility this can be a useful technique.

Take hold exactly as you would a pencil - you can allow either a sharp or rounded corner to protrude - and pivot the plectrum between your thumb and first and second fingers as shown. You can now control the stiffness by pressing a little with your thumb.

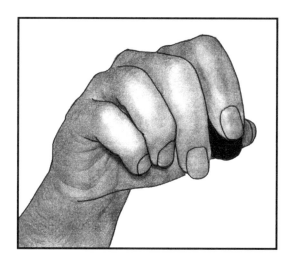

Figure 13

'Pencil grip' - the plectrum is anchored
between the thumb and first two fingers.

TREMOLO

Because this book isn't aimed at complete beginners, let's assume you've got a passable command of tremolo by now and have just a short recap before we look at some of the finer points of the technique. Tremolo is a rapid succession of identical notes giving the impression of a long, sustained note. Mandolins, particularly cheap ones, don't have as much sustain as, say, a violin, and this is the time-honoured way of compensating. So if a mandolinist comes across this:

Exercise 14

CD r

she might be tempted to play this instead:

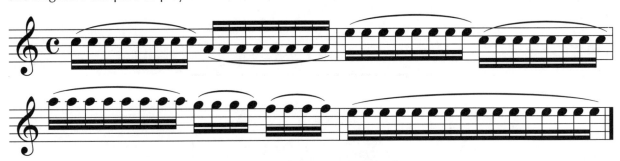

Incidentally, tremolo is never written out like this; we use the special slashes you can see in *Exercise 15* below, or sometimes we just make a note on the score.

Of course, the technique fools nobody. It sounds exactly like what it is: lots of little notes. At its worst it can sound like a machine gun going off, although with less dynamic range, but at its best it can be wonderfully expressive and has become the sound most associated with the mandolin in the ears of the general public.

Do I mention dynamics in jest? Only partly. The great danger with tremolo is that you reach a certain level of competence, in that your right arm is able to deliver a smooth, controlled flow of notes, but you haven't thought about expression. So as an exercise, it's worth using tremolo to play through some really simple tunes in your repertoire and making a conscious effort to incorporate any dynamics that take your fancy - even try it on the four open strings to begin with:

Exercise 15

CD

It's possible to tremolo from the wrist, but you'll get more dynamic range if you keep the wrist straight (but not tense) and tremolo from the elbow. Learning to execute a nicely controlled swell comes in very useful when we have two consecutive notes at the same pitch. Try this next phrase (play it all tremolo):

CD ref 64

Notice it's all on one string with just one position shift at the end of bar 6. Play the high *d'* as an extension (just stretch the fourth finger). In bars 2, 3, and 5 we have 'problem' notes; swell the first, dip the volume slightly and then push again into the second note, all without losing the tremolo.

If you've experimented with plectrums and the merits of pointed and rounded corners (see the section on the right hand), you may have discovered that it's easier to tremolo with a rounded corner; the plectrum gives less resistance this way. This doesn't mean it's always a desirable thing to do, as all the comments about tone I make in that section hold true for tremolo as well.

It's difficult to cross strings mid-flow without introducing an audible hiatus in the music. So, as above, you might find yourself shifting up and down one string rather than crossing strings. Have a look at the alternative fingerings for *Lovely on the Water*. The first tablature staff is how we might play it ordinarily, the second is how we might play it tremolo - all on one string. You'll find shifting position with the left hand is easier than crossing strings and keeping the tremolo smooth.

Lovely on the Water

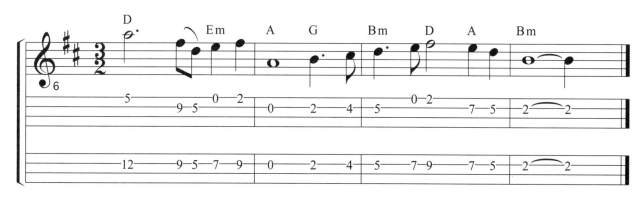

ref 65

trad arr S Mayor

Song of the Birds

Even when we've taken the decision to use tremolo for a tune, it's often not necessary or even desirable to use it throughout. What's more, from a practical point of view, taking a 'breath' gives us the chance to change strings should we need to. So, try using tremolo exactly as shown in this beautiful Spanish carol *Song of the Birds.* Remember to make it plain you've played two notes as you cross from bar 7 to bar 8, and again in bars 10 and 18. These last two instances will test your left hand control as you have to do a finger swap. The string numbers are shown in brackets.

CD ref 66

trad arr S Mayor

Lark in the Clear Air

trad arr S Mayor

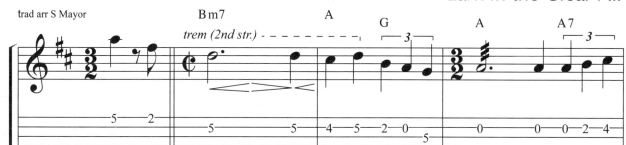

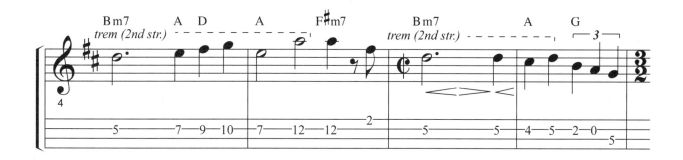

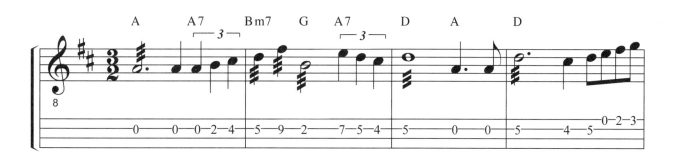

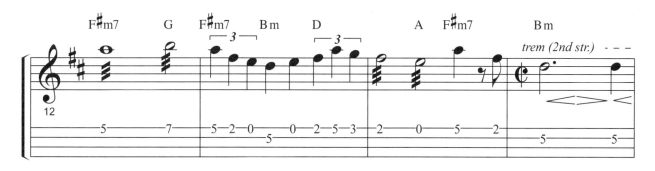

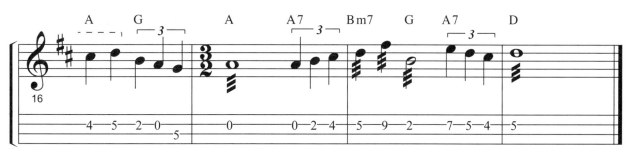

DOUBLE STOPPED TREMOLO

Playing double stopped tremolo is considerably harder than playing just a single line. This is not so much a right hand problem, you just have to widen your right arm movement a little and you should be able to take in two strings without much difficulty.

No, the left hand is more the worry. When we're trying to keep both a melody and a harmony line going at the same time it's inevitably going to involve more shifts and string crossings. Let's try some real Italian music for this most Italian of sounds.

Santa Lucia

trad arr S Mayor

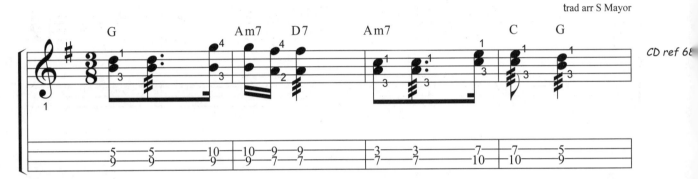

CD ref 68

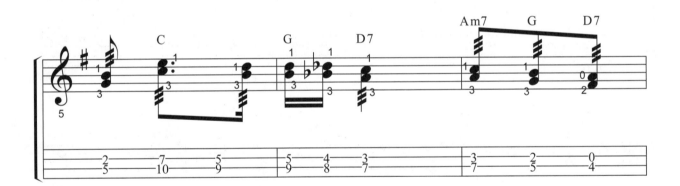

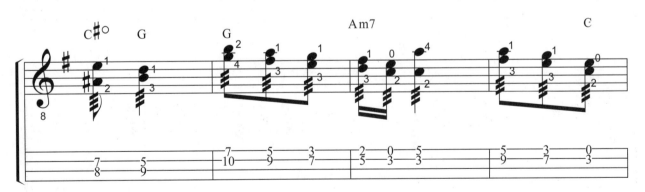

I've not indicated position shifts here, but if you follow the left hand fingerings closely, they should fall into place.

This isn't an easy piece to play smoothly, so don't be dispirited if it doesn't sound too good at first.

If you do nothing else, enjoy the final cheesy glissando!

BUNCHES & EXTENSIONS

So far we've considered how to use open strings to move out of first position, but there are other ways.

CD ref 69

In some keys there aren't that many open strings flying around, and if the tune involves moving up the neck we have to look for tricks to make the job as easy as possible. Take a close look at the fingering I've indicated for bars 7 - 9 of *Along The Grove*. The *c'* (3rd note in bar 8) is the crucial point: instead of using the second finger as might be expected, use the first. This is what I call *bunching* the left hand fingers. Here, they are hovering over frets 3 - 6, but only momentarily as the fourth finger has to reach immediately for the top *c'* (eighth fret, top string).

A similar thing happens a couple of notes later: instead of the second finger playing the *d'*, use the first, and again the left hand is bunched for a moment until the fourth finger reaches out for the top *d'* (tenth fret, top string).

The left hand has now shifted twice up to a closed position with the first finger over the fifth fret.

Along The Grove

S Mayor

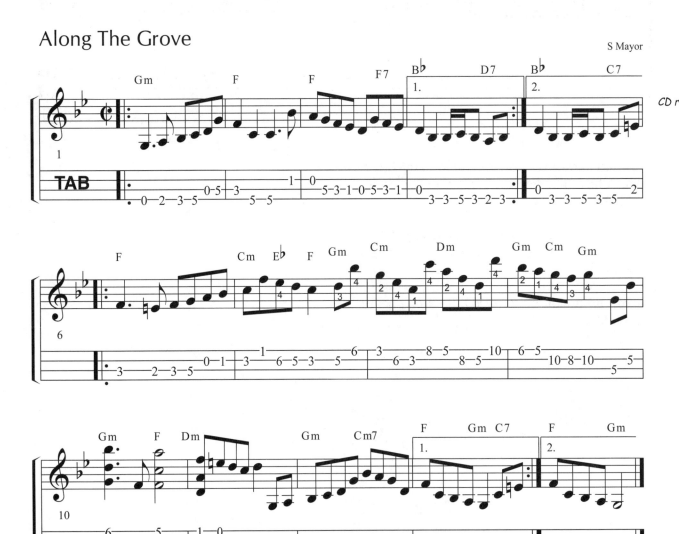

CD ref 70

Here's another example of some desirable bunching. This is the opening few bars of the third movement of *Vivaldi's Mandolin Concerto*. Look closely at the left hand fingering. In bars 1, 2 and 5 I've indicated the third finger on the high *g'* to leave the second finger free to nip in behind it and get the *c'*.

Similarly, in bars 3 and 4 the left hand is pulled back to what is sometimes called 'half' position. The second finger plays the *b'* leaving the first to play the *f'* on the top string.

(excerpt 3rd movt.) Vivaldi Mandolin Concerto

ref 71

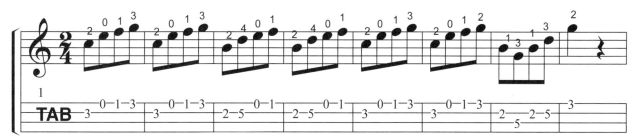

With the fingering to the right we have string jumping (the second finger at the end of bar 1 and the first finger at the end of bar 3). This may be a more obvious fingering but it introduces an almost unavoidable staccato effect.

this fingering is not recommended

Before we leave this phrase, below is another possible fingering that takes full advantage of the open *e'* string. It spreads the notes across adjacent strings but does involve the left hand in an 'extension' fingering: the three fret span between the first and second fingers in bars three and four. Look closely at both the tablature and left hand fingering here.

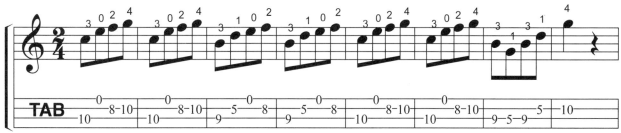

An extension is simply the opposite of a bunch. Whereas before the left hand fingers contracted and then expanded, now the opposite happens. First the fingers expand beyond the usual two-frets-per-finger span, then they contract again. Either way the left hand can move crab-like up and down the neck of the mandolin.

Some examples are overleaf.

Exercise 17

CD ref 72

You'll notice this exercise has alternative left hand fingerings. Above the notes (in the standard notation) is a bunched fingering, below the notes is an extended. Try them both; they are equally valid ways of tackling a passage like this.

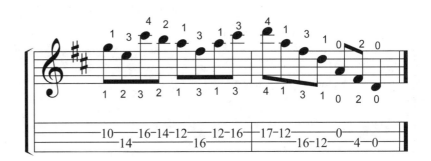

Vivaldi Mandolin Concerto *(excerpt 1st movt.)*

CD ref 7

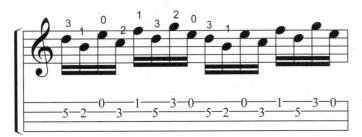

I use bunching to play this passage from the Vivaldi concerto (from the first movement this time). It features a sequence of rising sixths, a typical Vivaldi device which in this case ventures beyond first position on the mandolin.

The fingering shown allows this effect:

scrapbook

backstage with The Mandolinquents at the Theatre By The Lake, Keswick ...

... and enjoying the Autumn mist over Derwentwater the next morning

guesting with the American Guitar and Mandolin Summer School orchestra

an impromptu version of 'June Apple' with guitar ace Steve Kaufman

somewhere in there... with a truly international gathering of mandolinists at Rudolstadt Festival, Germany

HARMONIES AGAIN

Just when you thought your left hand had recovered from the previous sections on incorporating harmonies, here are two more tunes. I've saved them 'til now partly because I didn't want to overdose you earlier, and partly because these tunes work well as little solo pieces; guitar accompaniment is entirely optional.

The Captain's Apprentice

trad arr Simon Mayor

CD ref 7

This beautiful Scottish air was borrowed by Max Bruch for one of the main themes in his *Scottish Fantasy.* You may wish to try playing the simple version (just the upwards stems in the standard notation) as it's an ideal tune to try to maximise the sustain you can coax from your instrument without using tremolo.

For the full harmonised version, it's essential that you follow the left hand fingerings in the standard notation if you're going to be able to lend the piece a sense of flow. Play delicately, perhaps with the plectrum moved away from the bridge to get the sweeter tone over the end of the fingerboard.

MIND OVER MANDOLIN

Now a confession! I've never been one to subject myself to rigid practice routines as I've always so enjoyed playing the mandolin, on stage or off, that the thing is rarely out of my hands. So I do play a lot, and yes of course there are times where I'm in deep concentration trying out some new technique, trying to figure out how somebody did some dazzling lick, or writing a tune of my own.

But I've always found that a great way to get a piece totally and utterly under the fingers is to play it while I'm doing something else. Call it 'subliminal' practice if you like. Washing the dishes or mowing the lawn are both a little impractical in this regard, but try playing while you're watching the television. If you're like me, you'll wake up the next morning with the tune in your subsconcious just raring to go!

Of course, there are certain tunes that seem as if they were not only written for the mandolin, but written for our very fingers. Others seem to go fine, apart from one phrase that simply will not come clean whatever we try. While it's a perfectly common human condition to have a mental block about something, it's no less irritating.

If it happens to you, let me make you feel better; it happened to me with a tune I'd actually written *myself*. To be honest, I think I'd overplayed it. It was one of the first tunes I'd composed on the mandolin and I'd been playing it a long time, when I began to realise that I was consistently muffing a particular phrase on stage. It was crazy because the phrase isn't all that difficult - take a look on the opposite page at the rising triads in bars 6 and 7 of *Jump The Gun*.

I tried slowing the tune right down, and yes, of course I could play it slowly, but the next night on stage the same thing happened. My eventual solution was to change the way I thought; I broke down the phrase into logical, smaller parts - in this case a sequence of four rising triads - and created a 'shortcut' image in my mind. I gave myself four 'markers' to concentrate on: the first notes of each triad. I realised there was a simple upwards scale: *d'*, *e'*, *f#'*, and *g'*. So, I completely forgot about the fact that the phrase was a counter-rhythm to the main rhythm of the piece and I visualised the mandolin fingerboard and exactly what my left hand fingers were going to do as the phrase approached. If we were to notate it, this is what I saw in my mind's eye:

...and it worked!

I began to use this technique of visualisation regularly, not so much in places where I had a mental block about something simple (I'm fortunate in that it doesn't happen to me that often), but for passages that were just, well... difficult!

A typical situation would be a tune that stayed in first position for some time and then jumped into closed position, probably quite high up the neck. I'd make certain that I didn't expend any unnecessary concentration on the first position stuff, after all if I've got the gall to write instructional material I ought to be able to do that without thinking! Then I'd break down the difficult passage and take a mental 'snapshot' of where my fingers should be at the start of each lick within it. I'd tell myself that even if I did make mistakes, my fingers would be in their snapshot positions right on cue. Once again, it worked for me.

Jump The Gun

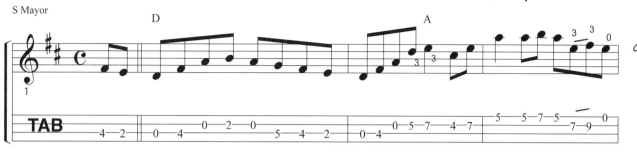

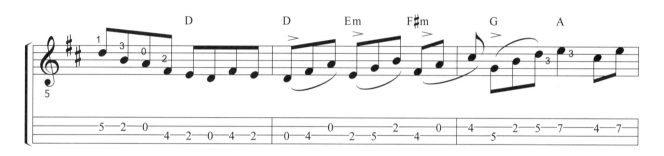

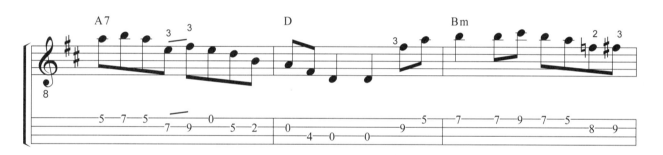

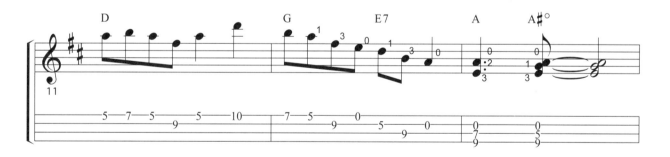

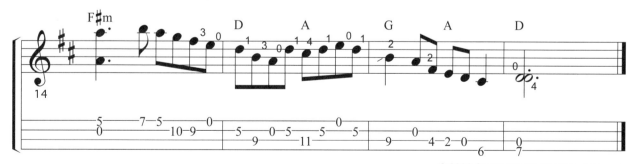

DUET

June Apple *(1st mandolin)*

trad arr S Mayor

CD ref 7

trad arr S Mayor

(2nd mandolin) June Apple

SWINGAROLA

S Mayor

CD ref 7

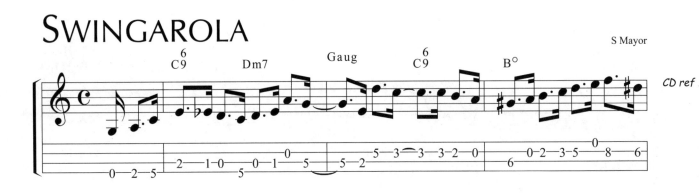

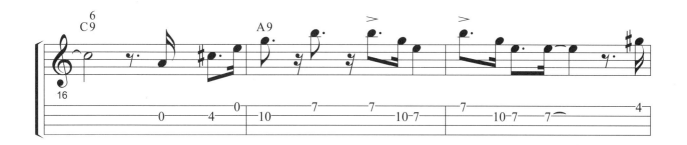

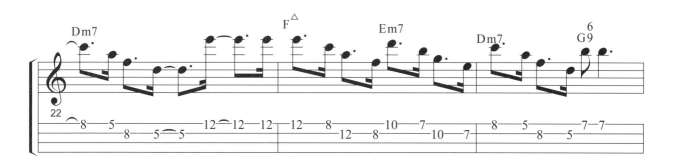
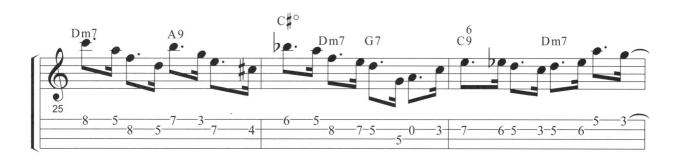
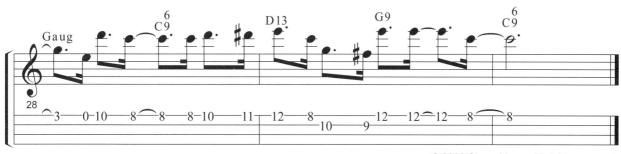

www.mandolin.co.uk

*visit Simon Mayor's website for up-to date news of new books, recordings, videos, DVDs and concert dates.
If you would like to receive a printed catalogue contact Acoustics at the address below.*

The Mandolin Album
CDACS 012

'Uplifting and a joy' DAILY TELEGRAPH

'Sheer joy' FOLK ROOTS

The Second Mandolin Album
CDACS 014

'Simply a masterpiece' TOWER RECORDS MAGAZINE

'Refreshing and uplifting' VOX

Winter With Mandolins CDACS 015

'Recording of the Week' BBC WORLD SERVICE

'The most beautiful bell-like mandolin sound I have ever heard' LIVING TRADITION

The English Mandolin
CDACS 025

'This is a delight, Simon Mayor's mandolin playing is without peer' FOLK ROOTS

New Celtic Mandolin CDACS 035

'A stunning album... the beauty of the slow airs along with the faster sets beggars belief' ROCK 'N' REEL

Mandolinquents CDACS 034

Hot swing and ragtime instrumentals, Irving Berlin, Mozart, Tchaikovsky, lively reels, beautiful Irish airs and Chinese and Brazilian folk tunes.

Duos CDACS 042
- live Simon Mayor & Hilary James

'Over [58] fretting, double-stringed minutes, give or take time off for demonstrations of similar fiddle and guitar expertise and some sweetly-sung blues, standards and folk songs from Hilary James, Simon Mayor takes the mandolin from hot-licking Texas fiddle tunes to Handel's Arrival of the Queen of Sheba played with blurry-fingered precision.' GLASGOW HERALD

New Celtic Mandolin *(book)*
ISBN 0-9522776-2-X

Thirty-one tunes from all corners of the Celtic World in standard notation and tablature with lots of technical tips and guitar chords. Includes arrangements for quartet and interviews with top players Andy Irvine, Maartin Allcock, Chris Newman, Gary Peterson and Brian Taheny. Includes all the tunes from Simon's New Celtic Mandolin CD.

The New Mandolin *(book)*
ISBN 0-9522776-0-3

Simon Mayor's book of 21 original tunes from his first three mandolin albums is laced with technical tips and humourous anecdotes.

The music is presented in standard notation and tablature and this updated edition now includes examples of harmony lines and quartet arrangements.

The Mandolin Tutor *(book/CD)*
ISBN 0-9522776-1-1   CDACS 028

A detailed course for beginners: tuning, right and left hand techniques, reading music & tablature, chords, tremolo, scales, exercises, tunes and simple duets, and advice on choosing & maintaining an instrument.

'It's way, way better than anything of this sort that I've seen.' FOLK ROOTS

Mandolin Essentials *(video)* VTACS 031

A learn-as-you-play approach for those in the early stages of mandolin playing. Simon s informal and encouraging style gets you playing five easy tunes in a variety of musical idioms, taking a detailed look at left hand fingering, right hand techniques, tips for making simple tunes sound more interesting, and lots, lots more.

New Celtic Mandolin *(video)* VTACS 032

For those who already know their way round the mandolin and want some expert advice and new ideas to spice up their playing of Celtic music. Simon Mayor takes a fresh and detailed look at five traditional and modern Celtic tunes, introducing original ideas and techniques that will benefit all aspects of mandolin playing.

Acoustics Records, PO Box 350, Reading RG6 7DQ, England.   tel: +44 (0)118 926 86
or order securely online at: www.acousticsrecords.co.uk